D1745431

THE POWER OF
CHEERFULNESS

Featuring the story of Bob Hope

Authors
Della Mae Rasmussen
Phyllis Colonna

Art Illustrator
Stephen P. Krause

Editor, Layout and Research
Beatrice W. Friel

THE POWER OF CHEERFULNESS

Featuring the story of Bob Hope

Advisors
Paul and Millie Cheesman
Mark Ray Davis
Rodney L. Mann, Jr.
Roxanne Shallenberger
Dale T. Tingey

Publisher
Steven R. Shallenberger

AN EAGLE SYSTEMS
INTERNATIONAL
PUBLICATION
ANTIOCH CALIFORNIA

Director and Correlator
Lael J. Woodbury

The Power of Cheerfulness
Copyright © 1981 by
PowerTales
Eagle Systems International
P.O. Box 1229
Antioch, California 94509

ISBN: 0-911712-83-0

Library of Congress Catalog No.: 80-85337

First Edition

Lithographed in USA by
COMMUNITY PRESS, INC.

Dedicated to people who choose to be happy, this tale is about a man
who chose to be cheerful, even when life was difficult.

BOB HOPE

Bob Hope was born 29 May 1903 in Eltham, a suburb of London, England. Named Leslie Townes Hope at birth, he was the fifth of seven boys. His father was a stonemason and his mother the daughter of a Welsh sea captain.

When Bob was about three, stonemason work became so scarce that Mr. Hope decided to go to America to join his two brothers who had settled in Cleveland. In 1908 Bob's mother and her sons joined Mr. Hope in America. Since work was still scarce, Bob's mother began taking in boarders and asked her sons to help with the family income whenever they could. As each son became old enough, he found odd jobs to supplement the family income.

By the time he was eight, Bob was singing on streetcars and at parks for spending money. As he grew older he not only sang, but he also worked as a newsboy, as a caddy, in a shoe store, in a meat shop, and for a motor company. He also enjoyed competing in races and amateur talent contests and often won prize money for his performances. His mother was his best fan and always supported and encouraged him.

Bob had a great love for the theater and the movies. His start in show business came from imitating his favorite actor, Charlie Chaplin. When he performed in vaudeville, his acts included singing, tap dancing, doing comedy sketches, and even playing the saxophone.

As time went on Bob became continually more involved in vaudeville. His stardom increased as he began appearing in Broadway shows and working in radio. Because of his successful radio broadcasts he was invited to appear in a Hollywood production, *The Big Broadcast of 1938*. In 1939 he had his first big screen hit, *The Cat and the Canary*. *Road to Singapore* was made in 1940 and was followed by six other "Road" pictures.

It was in 1933 that Bob met a young singer, Dolores Reade. They were married in 1934.

After their marriage Bob and Dolores made vaudeville and Broadway appearances together. Then she became more interested in her career as a wife and Bob returned to solo performing.

Because Dolores was unable to have children, the Hopes adopted an eight-week-old baby girl, Linda, in 1939. A year later a boy, Tony, was adopted. In 1946 they adopted two more children—a girl, Nora Avis, and a boy, Kelley.

Bob's screen comedy thrived through the forties, and he has continued making the public laugh in movies and TV appearances on into the eighties. He has made annual trips to entertain U.S. troops overseas.

Although he has been one of the world's busiest entertainers, he still found the time to write several humorous books about his career and travels.

At the age of seventy Bob was maintaining a schedule that would have tired a man half his age. Besides his regular television show and his annual USO tour, he was doing about ten college shows a year and countless benefits that took him to various parts of the country on a regular basis.

It has been said of Bob that he is "probably the richest entertainer who has ever lived." His wealth is estimated at between 400 and 700 million dollars, most of which is invested in real estate, securities, oil and gas wells, thoroughbred horses, a broadcasting company, and the Cleveland Indian baseball team.

Bob has won "special" Academy Awards five times for his humanitarian action and his contribution to the film industry. The following story is based on incidents in his life.

Hello!

Are you feeling cheerful today? I hope so! Did you know that cheerful people are healthier than gloomy people? Laughing and feeling happy are good for us!

Usually cheerful people are more successful than gloomy people, too. Would you rather buy something in a store where all the workers are happy or in a store where the workers are grouchy? Most of us like to buy from happy people. We like teachers who are cheerful, and we would rather work with someone who is in a good mood.

That's because happiness is contagious! When one person feels cheerful, other people catch it! Soon cheerfulness spreads through a whole crowd.

How do I know these things? I'm the Cheerful Chipmunk! My friends call me Chuck (short for Chuckle, you know). I want to tell you about a friend of mine named Bob Hope. For more than fifty years Bob has spread cheerfulness in almost every part of the world.

"Now just a minute, Chuck," I hear you saying. "I know all about Bob Hope. He's one of the richest men in Hollywood, and one of the most famous, too. No wonder he's cheerful!"

Well, that's true, but he wasn't always rich and famous. However he knew that cheerfulness isn't something that happens because everything is going right. He knew that cheerfulness is a way of looking at things, no matter how they are going!

Bob was born May 9, 1903, in London, England—one of the biggest and most famous cities in the world. His real name was Leslie Townes Hope. "Bob" is a nickname he earned when he came to America, but I'll tell you about that later. He had four older brothers when he was born, and later two other brothers were born into the family. You can imagine how lively things were with seven boys growing up together.

9

Bob's father had a good income when Bob was first born. He worked as a stonemason.

Not many years ago a stonemason was a very important man. He knew how to cut and shape stones, then fit them together to build houses, churches, and other buildings. But soon people began to build with brick, and stonemasons no longer had enough work to do. That's what happened to Bob's father. His income dropped from very good to very bad in only a few years. Mr. Hope could have acted sad and grouchy. Instead he cheerfully started looking for ways to solve his problems.

One day he received an exciting letter in the mail. "This letter is from my brother in America," he told his wife Avis. "He says his family really likes living there. These are hard times for us in England. I'm going to see if America is a good place for us to live, too."

So Mr. Hope set out across the ocean to look for new opportunities. "I don't know what kind of work I'll find, but I'll bet I can find something," he said. He knew that an important part of being cheerful is expecting things to work out well. Sure enough, he found a job soon after he arrived. He saved his money, and in a few months his wife and sons joined him in the new country.

They arrived on a cold, windy day in March 1908, but they were so happy to be together again that no one grumbled or complained. In fact, Mr. and Mrs. Hope didn't believe in grumbling or complaining. "It never makes things better," Mrs. Hope said, "and quite often it makes things worse."

Everyone in the family learned a lot about being cheerful from Avis Hope. She was a tiny woman, but she was big enough for any task she decided to do. She was happy and energetic in her work, and things got done right when she did them. She was very proud of her seven sons. "You are the most marvelous boys any mother could want," she told them. "I just know you'll make a success of anything you decide to do." No wonder they felt cheerful.

Mrs. Hope loved music and laughter. While the family was living in Cleveland, Ohio, she bought a piano—even though there was scarcely enough money for shoes. "We will find ways to get the other things we need," she said with a smile. "Music is important. Every family should have singing and laughter in the home."

Her friends said, "Avis Hope has learned to walk on the bright side of life."

She could have been very discouraged. Getting settled in a new country takes time, and at first the Hope family had very little money. But Mrs. Hope believed in solving problems and not being sad about them. She called her sons for a family council.

"Your father works hard to earn the money we need," she said. "We all need to find ways to help. I have decided to take in boarders. They will pay us to live in our home and eat the meals I fix. What ways can you find to earn extra money?"

Do you think the boys grumbled and complained at the thought of working after school instead of playing with their friends? If you do, you're wrong. They had learned that if you look on the bright side of things, you can find ways to enjoy whatever you're doing. They started looking for odd jobs to help pay the family bills.

Bob found many ways he could earn money. He sold newspapers, worked in a butcher shop, helped sell shoes, worked in a store, and carried golf clubs at the local golf course. Everywhere he went he made friends and learned interesting things. He learned to play golf so well that it became a lifelong favorite sport.

Of course Bob found ways to earn money for his own entertainment, too. In Cleveland the boys his age liked going to Luna Park, an amusement park. Although Bob was only eight years old, he found an unusual way to pay for his ticket and the rides and games inside.

"Let's take the streetcar to Luna Park," he often told his friends. When the streetcar was on its way, Bob would sing to the passengers. Sometimes the other boys would sing, too. Then one of them would pass his hat around for people to drop coins in. The passengers were glad for the entertainment, and the boys were glad to have money to spend at the park. If they ran short before they were ready to go home, they stopped on a street corner and sang more songs.

THINK ABOUT IT

1. Bob's family worked hard, but they believed in enjoying life, too. How did this help Bob learn to be cheerful?
2. Do you think being cheerful helped Bob think of ways to earn money?
3. Is it easier to solve problems and come up with new ideas when you are happy or when you are sad?

BOB GOES INTO SHOW BUSINESS

Bob liked to sing for people. In fact, he enjoyed show business of all kinds. Whenever he could, he went to see variety shows at the local theaters. He liked to watch different actors sing and dance, and he liked the funny stories they told to make people laugh.

"I'll bet I could do that," he thought to himself. "People like to hear me sing, and they laugh at my jokes. Maybe I'll enter the next amateur night contest. I might even win a prize!"

And that's what he did. He entered and won. He thought, "That was easy! I think I'll enter more singing contests." He discovered that the more he performed for people, the more he enjoyed it. He liked the money he earned, and he liked the applause.

Bob had a good friend called Whitey Jenkins. Whitey had ideas for making extra money, too. "You're good at winning contests," he said to Bob one day. "Can you run fast? Some of the big companies hold picnics for their workers at the park. Sometimes they have races and other contests. Maybe we could win some prize money." The two friends began entering races, and often they won. "It's great to earn money," Bob said. "It's even better to earn it doing something you like." He knew that an important part of being cheerful is looking for things you like to do and things you can do well.

Bob liked sports, especially outdoor sports like running and golfing. It's a good thing he kept in shape because when he first moved to Cleveland he had a big problem to solve. In England he was taught proper manners. He was taught to dress in proper English clothes, too, with a broad Eton collar and a long flowing tie. Even his English accent sounded strange to the boys at his new American school. They formed a circle around him on the playground.

"What's your name?" they asked. Bob answered as he had been taught to answer in England, giving his last name first. "Hope, Leslie," he told them. The American boys doubled up with laughter. "Hope-Leslie . . . hopelessly . . . you really are hopeless, aren't you?" they mocked.

But Bob was not afraid to stand up for himself, even if he was the only one to do it. After a few school yard battles the other boys admitted that "Hope, Leslie," was no sissy. From then on everyone called him Bob. He liked the new name and even used it himself. Bob never held grudges, so soon he had many new friends. "I can't be cheerful and angry at the same time," he said. "I choose to be cheerful."

Little by little, Bob was finding out what he really enjoyed in life. He liked friendly, happy people. He liked the theater and singing. He liked applause and the good feeling he got when he knew he had performed well. He liked winning contests and earning money, too. He used money wisely, and from the time he had his first job, no matter how much or how little he earned, he always saved some of it.

There was something else Bob discovered that he liked. Movies were beginning to be popular, and Bob enjoyed movies almost as much as he liked vaudeville. Whenever he had an extra dime, he sat in the dark theater and watched the famous actors, especially the comedians. His favorite was a strange little man named Charlie Chaplin. Chaplin had a black mustache, and he always wore a baggy suit. Bob laughed at him so hard his sides ached when the movie was over.

"I wish I could make people laugh like he does," Bob thought to himself. "A few years ago no one knew his name. Now he's the world's most famous comedian. I wonder if I could learn some of his routines."

Bob borrowed a baggy suit from his older brother and a derby hat from his father. He painted a mustache under his nose with stove blacking and made a cane out of a tree limb. Soon he looked like Charlie Chaplin's twin brother. When he waddled down the street in Chaplin's funny duck walk, people stopped whatever they were doing and stared. Everywhere Bob went people laughed and laughed.

Bob's brothers thought he was so good they decided to enter him in a Charlie Chaplin look-alike contest at Luna Park. When the judge asked the people in the audience what they thought of Bob's performance, they wouldn't stop clapping and cheering. Bob even made a joke out of that. "It's easy to win contests when you have six brothers in the audience," he said. "Six brothers can make a lot of noise."

By the time he was a teenager, Bob had decided show business was his chosen future. "The actors are cheerful and fun to be with," he told his family. "They make other people feel happy, too."

He started his career by playing parts in vaudeville—a theater where actors sing and dance, play musical instruments, and entertain the audience with jokes and funny stories. Bob was good at all these things. But the jokes he told were never mean or sarcastic. Even when he made fun of someone, he was good-humored. Most of his jokes were about himself. For instance, he liked to make fun of his long nose that turned up at the end. He called it a ski-jump nose.

"I went to Hollywood to take a screen test the other day," he told his audience. "I was awful. My nose came onto the screen ten minutes before the rest of my face."

Many of his jokes were so old that they were awful too, but for some reason, when Bob told them, they were funny.

"Doctor, will I be able to play the piano when my broken hand gets better?" he asked in one scene.

"Yes, of course you will," the doctor answered.

"That's great!" Bob said. "I could never play it before."

Bob liked acting in vaudeville very much. "I'm doing what I like best, and I'm earning $40 a week besides," he told his family. "Imagine getting paid to make people laugh!"

Soon Bob was getting paid much more than $40 a week. People liked this cheerful young man who made them forget their problems for awhile. In fact, they liked him so much he was asked to perform at the Palace, the most important vaudeville theater in New York. That was only the beginning of his success. At the Palace he was so popular that he was given a part in a big Broadway musical.

The musical was called *Roberta*. It was another great hit for Bob, and for the first time in his life, he was rich. He bought the fanciest, most expensive car he could find—a Pierce Arrow. "I must be the luckiest man in the world," he said jokingly. "I am young and good-looking. I have money and friends. I even have a Pierce Arrow! What more could I want?" But, as a matter of fact, something very important was still missing in his life.

One night a friend took him to hear a young woman sing. Her name was Dolores Reade, and the song she sang was called "Did You Ever See a Dream Walking?" Bob thought Dolores was the dream in the song. He told his friend, "I have to meet that girl! Find someone to introduce me!" A few months later he and Dolores were married.

They were a very happy couple, and they often worked together. Dolores sang beautiful songs while Bob made the audience laugh by flirting with her and making funny faces. Bob had a popular radio show, too, and more and more people asked him to be in their Broadway shows. When he had extra time, he went back to play in vaudeville. His earnings jumped from $40 a week to $5,000 a week.

Bob became so popular that Paramount Studios asked him to come to Hollywood. Even though people liked the movies he made, Bob knew the parts he played weren't very good. Paramount didn't think he was important enough to have starring roles. But he made movies with some of the most famous actors of that time—Martha Raye, Betty Grable, George Burns, and Gracie Allen.

Then something happened to make them change their minds. Pepsodent Toothpaste Company asked Bob to star in a comedy show for radio. It became so popular that soon everyone was talking about "Mr. Pepsodent." When Paramount Studios saw that Bob had become famous, they arranged to give him some starring roles.

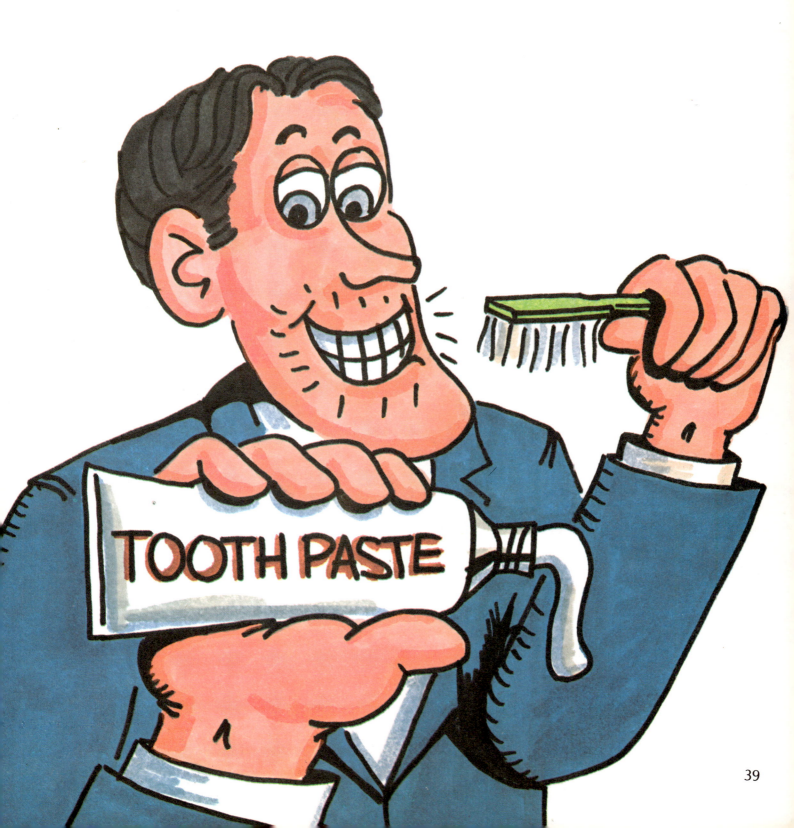

They made a suspense comedy called *The Cat and the Canary*. Paulette Goddard, a beautiful star, played the part of the leading lady. She was supposed to be in great danger and Bob was supposed to protect her. The movie was funny because Bob was more afraid than Paulette was.

The Cat and the Canary convinced Paramount Bob should star in more movies. One day they told him, "We've scheduled you with two of the biggest names in Hollywood—Bing Crosby and Dorothy Lamour! We're calling the movie *The Road to Singapore*."

Bob could scarcely believe his good luck. "What a break! Bing Crosby and Dorothy Lamour!" he thought. "I know they're famous, but are they fun to work with? I wonder if they'll like working with me."

They did like working with Bob. In fact, the three of them became one of the most famous teams in Hollywood. *The Road to Singapore* was so successful that Paramount began a whole series of Road movies, including *The Road to Zanzibar, The Road to Rio, The Road to Utopia, The Road to Morocco,* and several others. Bob, Bing, and Dorothy had so much fun working together that everyone who saw their movies felt happy for days. That's what I mean by cheerfulness being contagious!

Bob and Bing were not only funny together, they became best friends. They were both good at making up jokes as they went along. In fact, they made up jokes so fast that the other actors could hardly play their parts without laughing. The cameraman thought the jokes were so funny that he made them a part of the finished movie.

For instance, in *The Road to Morocco* Bob and Bing had a big scene with a camel. Now if you know about camels, you know that quite often they are grumpy and bad-tempered. Whenever they get a chance, they like to bite people or spit on them.

The camel in *The Road to Morocco* was supposed to sneak up behind Bob and Bing and lick their faces. They thought a beautiful girl was trying to give them a kiss, but when they turned around they were staring into the face of the camel. The camel decided to add his own part—he spit in Bob's face, Bob staggered backward, gasping for breath, while Bing doubled-up laughing. The cameraman just kept rolling the film.

Bob was the only person on the set who wasn't laughing. He was having too much trouble breathing. "You wouldn't believe how much chewed-up hay a camel can hide in its cheek," he said later. "I thought I'd been hit by the whole Casbah Garbage Department."

The Road to Morocco was another hit. Many people asked the cameraman, "How did you get that camel to spit at just the right minute?" He answered, "I worked with that beast for weeks to get him to spit on signal!" But Bob and Bing knew that the scene was the camel's own idea.

THINK ABOUT IT

1. Why do you think the cameramen and other actors liked to work with Bing and Bob?
2. How would that make their movies more successful?
3. Can you think of a time you were around people who were having a good time doing their work? How did you feel?

BOB AND DOLORES ADOPT A FAMILY

Bob liked his work more and more each year. He and Dolores enjoyed living in Hollywood, but they had one great disappointment in life. As the years passed they discovered they could never have children. This disappointment could have saddened the rest of their lives, but Bob had learned long ago to face his problems as cheerfully as possible.

"I always wanted a large family," Bob told Dolores. "My brothers and I had such good times growing up together. We always stood up for each other, and what one of us couldn't think of, another one could."

"You'd be a good father," Dolores said. "Why don't we adopt a baby? I know we'd love it as much as any parents love their children."

At first Bob was worried about that idea. "What if it doesn't work out?" he asked. "What if we change our minds later?" Dolores just laughed. She knew that would never happen.

Sure enough, when they finally brought their baby daughter home for the first time, Bob was as proud as any father could be.

"Look at her!" he said to Dolores. "Did you ever see an eight-week-old kid with so much personality?"

Little Linda did have personality. She was so cheerful and good-tempered that Bob and Dolores decided another baby would be no trouble at all. Within a year a little brother, Tony, was adopted into the family.

Bob and Dolores really enjoyed their growing children. After a few years had passed, Bob said, "This house is getting too quiet. Don't you think we need another baby?"

This time the adoption agency gave them a choice between a baby boy and a baby girl. Dolores didn't know what to do. She kept going from one crib to the other. "But I knew what to do," Bob said. "While she was trying to make up her mind, I signed the papers for both of them!"

Now Bob, Dolores, and their four children were a large, happy family. "Do you still think you might change your mind?" Dolores teased him while riding home on the train. Just then one of the porters came through their car. "Those are the best babies I ever saw!" he told them. "And doesn't that little boy look like his daddy!" Bob just grinned.

Bob was still making popular movies for Paramount. He had to do dangerous stunts in some of them. In *The Road to Utopia* he and Bing were stranded in a cabin in Alaska. They were supposed to go to sleep in the cabin, then in the night a bear was to come in and join them.

"Are you sure that bear's tame?" Bob asked the animal trainer. "Oh yes," he answered. "As tame as a kitten."

Bob and Bing went into the cabin and pretended to be asleep. Soon they could hear the bear sniffing around their heads. Then they heard a deep growl.

"Do you hear what I hear?" Bing whispered.

"I sure do," Bob whispered back. "Lead the way, Dad!"

They were so scared they probably set a world's record for leaping out of bed.

"That's it with the bear!" Bing told the director, and Bob backed him all the way. The next day they heard that same bear tore his trainer's arm off.

"Some kitten!" Bob said.

In the movie *Fancy Pants* Bob was surrounded by stunt men dressed as Indians. They were throwing arrows and hatchets all around him.

"They came so close they almost turned my ski-jump nose into a runaway sled. I could have won an Oscar for terror!" Later he said, "I've done a lot in this business for the sake of Art—and if I ever find him, I'll murder him!"

Bob was told to play the part of a swashbuckler in *Casanova's Big Night*. "I had a little trouble with that role," he said. "Everytime I was supposed to swash, I buckled."

In another movie called *Bachelor in Paradise,* Bob put too much detergent in the washing machine and the house filled up with suds. He called the fire department for help.

"Where's the fire?" the fireman asked.

"No fire," Bob answered.

"Then why did you call the fire department?" the fireman asked.

"If I hollared 'Soap!' who'd come?" Bob answered.

Bob made more than seventy movies. Wherever they were shown, people crowded into the theaters to see them. "People like a good laugh," Bob said. "It's good to forget the day's troubles and be cheerful for awhile."

Bob had come a long way since he sang for nickles and dimes on the streetcar in Cleveland. He was a vaudeville star, then a Broadway star, then a Hollywood movie star, and then a television superstar. But there was one role that meant more to him than any other.

Whenever America had soldiers and sailors in other countries, Bob was nearby putting on shows for them. In thirty years he traveled more than six million miles. Sometimes he was very close to the front lines where the fighting was. The soldiers called him "America's No. 1 soldier in greasepaint." After putting on a show for the combat soldiers, Bob always visited the hospitals. Often he would stop to put his arm around a wounded man and have a picture taken for him to send home to his family. "Did you see my show?" he often asked. "Or were you sick already?"

Bob has become well-known to almost every American. "You'd never guess he is almost 80 years old," one of his friends said not long ago. "He still plays golf. He still likes to keep in good shape. He never seems to get any older."

"After golf, Bob's favorite game is monopoly—but he plays with real money," one magazine wrote. It's true that Bob is very rich—one of the richest men in show business history. But he remains as cheerful and good-humored as when he was a young boy. He still saves part of everything he makes, too! He uses money wisely.

Bob's talent and his cheerful good humor are so famous that he has been asked to perform in the White House for many presidents of the United States. In 1977 he was invited to take part in the Queen's Jubilee in England. President Reagan once called him "England's most successful export."

"I make jokes about people and things I really care about," Bob said. "I've made jokes about the President, our country, golf, and even Bing Crosby. It doesn't hurt to laugh about serious things if you do it in the right spirit."

"I make fun of movies and show business, too, but I'm proud to be part of it all. I walk down a street in Paris or Manila and some kid takes one look at my ski-jump nose—'Hey, there's Bob Hope!' he hollers. It still makes me feel good after all these years."

Bob has won many contests and many prizes—for singing, for running, for acting, for community service. If there was one big international prize for spreading cheerfulness, he would win that too!